THEY SWIM THE SEAS

THEY SWIM

THE SEAS

THE MYSTERY OF ANIMAL MIGRATION

by Seymour Simon   *illustrated by* Elsa Warnick

Browndeer Press
Harcourt Brace & Company

San Diego   New York   London

For my grandchildren,
Joel, Benjamin, and Chloe, with love
—S. S.

For Jack and Fred
and our loving memories
of Alan, Mom, and Dad
—E. W.

Text copyright © 1998 by Seymour Simon
Illustrations copyright © 1998 by Elsa Warnick

Browndeer Press is a registered trademark of Harcourt Brace & Company.

Library of Congress Cataloging-in-Publication Data
Simon, Seymour.
They swim the seas: the mystery of animal migration/by Seymour Simon;
illustrated by Elsa Warnick.
p.   cm.
"Browndeer Press."
Summary: Describes the migration of marine animals and plants
as they journey through rivers, seas, and oceans.
ISBN 0-15-292888-X
1. Marine organisms—Juvenile literature.   2. Marine animals—
Migration—Juvenile literature.   [1. Marine animals.   2. Marine plants.]
I. Warnick, Elsa, ill.   II. Title.
QH91.16.S57   1998
578.77—dc21   97-4292

First edition
F E D C B A

Printed in Singapore

The oceans cover almost three-quarters of the world, yet only the smallest fraction of the water is visible. Underneath the oceans' windblown surfaces the waters go down to an average depth of sixteen thousand feet. The deepest parts of the seas stretch about seven miles below the surface. Mount Everest, the highest mountain on the land, could easily disappear below the waves in those depths. The sun lights the surface waters of the seas during the day, but its rays cannot penetrate below a depth of a few hundred feet, and the deeper ocean waters are sunless all the time.

Waves, tides, and currents constantly keep the waters in motion. In the life of a water animal or plant, movement is natural; remaining in one place requires more effort than moving. Partly because of this, nearly all fish go on journeys, as do most other sea animals and sea plants.

The watery world is in many ways similar to the mixture of gases we call the atmosphere. Water has "winds" in the form of currents, and there are "fronts" between warm and cold water, just as there are between warm and cold air masses. Currents flow up and down as well as side to side. Freshwater animals living in rivers and lakes are also affected by currents, though currents in small lakes are usually much weaker than those in huge seas.

Fish are more abundant in the earth's waters than any other good-sized animals. They are found all over the world—in salty oceans and seas and in freshwater lakes, rivers, streams, ponds, and swamps. In fact, there are as many different species of fish as there are of mammals, birds, reptiles, and amphibians put together.

Fish usually have gills that allow them to breathe the oxygen dissolved in water. They are also cold-blooded, which means their body temperature is nearly the same as the temperature of their surroundings. The bodies of most fish are covered with scales, a layer of protective bony or horny plates in overlapping rows. Some fish, such as eels, have scales that are very tiny and difficult to see.

Most fish have streamlined shapes that allow them to move through the water rapidly. The rear end of the body moves from side to side, pushing the fish through the water. The fins act as stabilizers and fine-tune the movements, allowing the fish to move up and down, as well as side to side and forward and backward.

$\mathcal{P}$lants need water to live and many of them also journey in water. Nonflowering plants, such as seaweeds, are often broken or torn by waves along shores, and their pieces are carried away by ocean currents to grow in different places. Freshwater nonflowering plants, such as an alga called spirogyra, also break apart and are spread by the moving waters of streams and ponds.

Flowering seashore plants often have seeds that float and are protected from salt water by a tough coat or shell. The seeds sprout when they come to rest on a warm, sandy shore. One such plant, the beach morning glory, grows throughout the Tropics along the high-tide line.

The coconut palm produces huge nuts that are covered with a fibrous husk, which helps to protect the nuts and also allows them to float in seawater. The nut is really a seed, and when it is washed up on a distant sandy beach it may germinate and give rise to a new palm tree.

Plankton is the name given to very tiny animals and plants that drift in oceans and lakes. Their name comes from a Greek word meaning "wandering" or "drifting." Most plankton are smaller than the head of a pin. Many are too small to be seen without a microscope, but some, such as large jellyfish, are nearly ten feet long. The numbers of plankton are enormous, and they serve as the main source of food for fish and other larger water animals.

The journeys of some plankton are like daily elevator rides: They travel up in the water during the night and down during the day. Some kinds of plankton seem to be on an express, riding up or down more than three thousand feet twice a day. Other kinds of plankton seem to be on a local, riding only three hundred feet up and down on their daily odysseys.

As the daylight fades and dusk comes to the sea, the plankton begin their rise to the surface. When the sun rises and the day dawns, the plankton return to the depths.

Predators often hunt in the surface waters during the day when they can see their prey. Because animal plankton usually remain in the dark depths during the day and move upward only at night, they have a better chance of survival.

At high tide on a remote ocean island on a warm spring night, large shadowy forms roll in with the breaking waves. In the silvery moonlight the head of a reptile can be seen rising out of the water, turning to peer in all directions. For several minutes the glistening boxlike creature remains in the line of breakers, water streaming over its shell. Having determined that there is no danger, the giant sea turtle moves its flippers and struggles onto the sandy beach. The sea turtle has returned to its nesting place after several years and a journey of thousands of miles.

The ocean journeys of sea turtles are truly amazing. Green turtles, which may weigh as much eight hundred pounds, live solitary lives when they are adults, feeding on seaweed and sea grasses and growing larger and larger. Then every two to eight years, both males and females begin the lonely journey to a breeding area in the ocean sixty miles from Ascension Island, fourteen hundred miles from their homes off the coast of Brazil. After mating, the males return to the distant feeding areas, while the females swim toward the waters near the Ascension Island nesting beaches. Here the female green turtle begins to produce eggs, then fertilizes them using sperm—from the male turtles—she has stored in her body.

After about four weeks the female turtle is ready to lay her first clutch of eggs. Shortly after sunset she climbs the beach in search of a patch of sand in which to dig a nest cavity. Using her flippers as shovels, she digs a hole about three feet deep, reaching sand that will remain at a constant temperature and moisture level. She then lays about one hundred eggs, covers them with sand, and returns to the sea. Several thousand turtles may lay eggs on one beach at the same time, and many millions of eggs are laid over an entire nesting season.

At the end of the breeding season, the females return to their home feeding grounds. The same female turtle may not breed again for two to eight years. If the female lives long enough and if the breeding beaches are still available, she may repeat her migration many times during her decades-long life.

The eggs remain incubating in the wet sand, warmed by the sun. After they hatch, baby turtles about as big as the palm of a person's hand struggle to the surface of the beach, usually during the night. Then they march directly into the sea and swim rapidly away from land. Before they reach the water, a few hatchlings are taken by birds, crabs, and other animals. But it is in the offshore waters that they are in the most danger, from sharks and other fish.

Only after several days of frantic swimming do the hatchlings rest, among drifting mats of seaweed, and begin to feed on animal plankton. For several years the young turtles feed and grow as they drift along with the ocean currents. In time they find their way to the feeding areas fourteen hundred miles away, where they will spend the rest of their adult lives, except for breeding seasons.

The open waters of the ocean are filled with large, swiftly moving shoals (or large schools) of herring. Their silvery bodies glint in the sunlight and ripple the surface waters like a passing wind. Each day the schools of herring migrate to the surface and down again following the movements of the plankton on which they feed. Over the course of a year, the herring migrate seasonally in large circles following ocean currents, from feeding to spawning to wintering grounds.

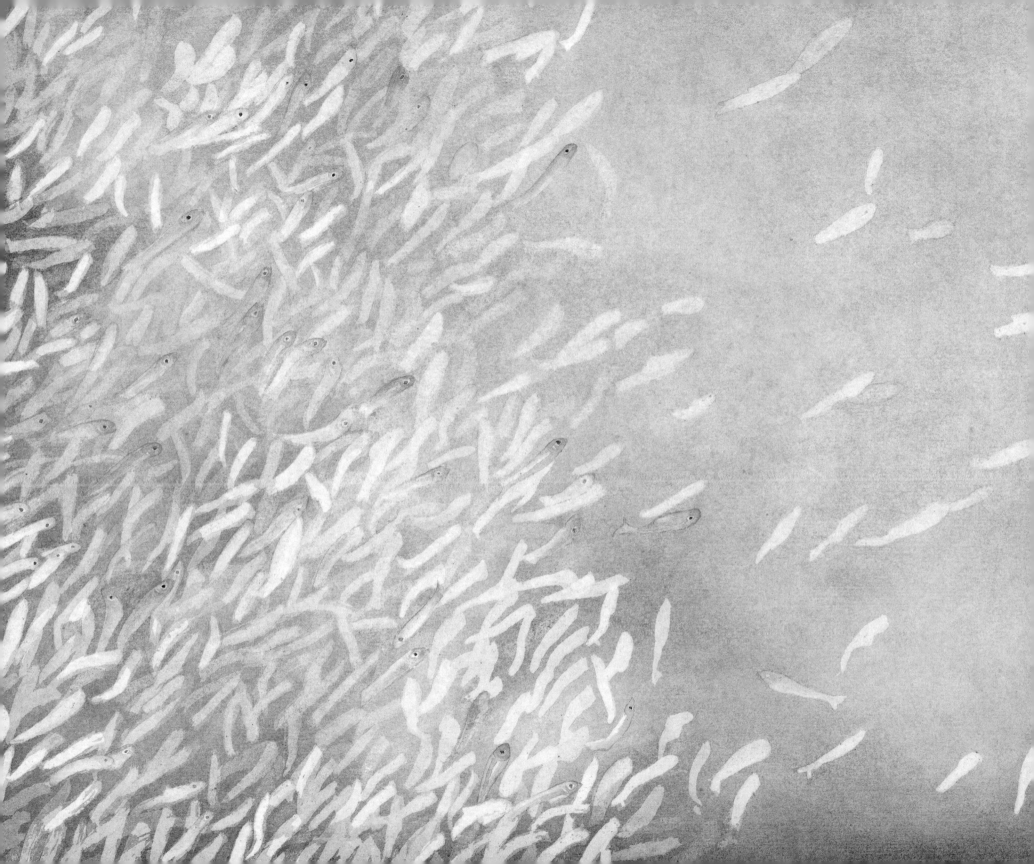

Tuna are true oceanic fish. Their streamlined bodies are fashioned to slip through the water with a minimum of effort. The fastest of all fish, tuna can reach bursts of speed greater than fifty miles per hour and can "cruise" at five to ten miles per hour for months without resting.

Like packs of undersea wolves, schools of tuna relentlessly pursue schools of the smaller fish and squid on which they feed. Their speed and the huge distances they cover make the tuna difficult for scientists to study. How can scientists follow a tagged fish that is traveling three times faster than the boat from which it is being observed?

Tuna migrate through most of the world's seas. Different populations migrate to their spawning grounds at different times. The eggs and newly hatched tuna drift for a few days before the young begin to swim and to form schools. For the next few years the schools of young tuna swim and feed. When they mature they head for waters in polar areas, where they spend most of their lives. Once a year some of the adults head in large schools to warmer waters to spawn.

How do tuna find their way to the same spawning grounds where they were born? No one really knows. Perhaps tuna, like other fish, have senses we are unaware of, which allow them to read signs in their watery world that we cannot see.

The Sargasso Sea is a free-floating "meadow" of seaweed, almost as large as a continent, lying south of Bermuda in the North Atlantic Ocean. Scientists know that North American and European eels spawn in the Sargasso Sea, yet no adult eel has ever been caught there. And even though scientists know much about the life story of eels, their long journeys to and from the Sargasso Sea remain one of the most mysterious of all animal migrations.

We know that all eels lay their eggs in ocean waters. The young are flat and transparent and hardly look like eels at all. These creatures, sometimes called leaf fish, are only two or three inches long and can be found only in the oceans. They cannot survive in freshwater.

Yet two of the best known species
of eels, the American eel and the European eel, are found
in the Sargasso Sea only when they are young, and are
found in freshwater lakes, rivers, and streams only
when they are adult.

In the autumn of each year large adult female eels
(which can be up to six feet long) of both Atlantic species
migrate to the coast from freshwater lakes and rivers, entering
the sea and joining the males who normally live in coastal waters.

In Europe and in America, hundreds of millions
of eels migrate down rivers, pour into
the ocean, and swim onward until
they leave the coastal waters.
Then they completely
disappear.

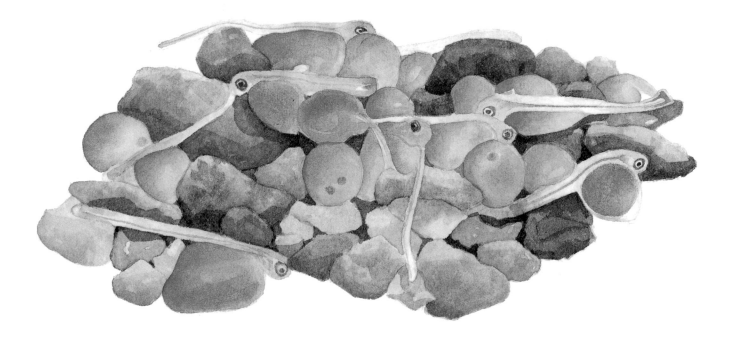

The life journey of the salmon begins when the female buries several thousand fertilized eggs in a shallow nest dug in the gravel bottom of a cool stream. After several months the eggs hatch. Each young salmon, or alevin, has a large, bright orange yolk sac attached to its body. The alevins remain in the gravel for another month, until the food stored in the yolk sac is exhausted. Then the young fry wriggle away from the sac and swim to the surface.

Leaving the safety of their freshwater homes, the growing salmon, now known as smolts, begin their dangerous journeys downriver to the ocean. Along the way they run a gauntlet of predators, such as birds and larger fish. The journey is even more dangerous when there are dams along the way; many smolts are swept into the turbines and killed. Finally countless millions of silvery smolts reach the sea.

After about four years, in the spring and summer, the mature adults return to coastal waters to begin their homeward journey. On their way back to their spawning sites, Pacific salmon may travel as many as several thousand miles to reach the coast.

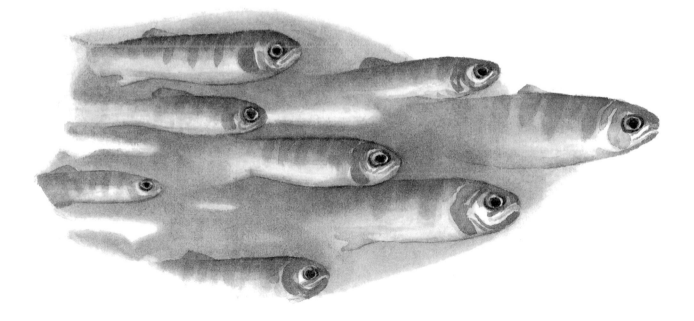

The mature salmon now begin to show the dramatic red colors of spawners. When they leave the ocean they are strong and healthy and have large reserves of fat in their bodies. After they enter freshwater, the fish eat nothing. The returning salmon leap over ten-foot-high waterfalls, jump and splash across churning rapids, and wriggle across shallow beds of stones. Many are caught by the brown bears that lie in wait for them along the stream beds.

As the salmon fight their way upstream, the jaws of the males develop into powerful toothed hooks, which they will soon use as weapons against other males in savage battles for a mate.

By the time they arrive in their home waters the salmon are thin and tired and their fat reserves are used up. They spawn and a few days later will die. But not before their fertilized eggs have been placed in nests among the rocks, and the life cycle of the salmon has begun once again.

Seals are born on land or on floating ice islands but spend much of their lives in the sea. Many of these furry mammals don't travel very far, but some of them range widely from their birthplaces.

Elephant seals are the largest of the seals; males can weigh more than five thousand pounds and can reach a length of eighteen to twenty feet—as big as an automobile. The elephant seal's name comes not just from its large size, but also from its long nose, which looks something like an elephant's trunk. Elephant seals like to swim and eat. They hold their breath when they dive.

Female elephant seals swim great distances to feed and do not seem to follow a regular path. Male elephant seals, on the other hand, often follow a regular yearly route. For example, northern elephant seal males swim from breeding areas in Baja California as far north as the coast of Washington State every year, where they feed at depths of over one thousand feet, eating slow-moving fish as well as small sharks and squid. Southern elephant seal males migrate in a circular path around the south pole through Antarctic waters.

Among sea mammals, the great migrators are the whales. Unlike seals and other sea mammals, whales spend their entire lives in water. All kinds of whales migrate. Some take yearly round-trip journeys that are thousands of miles long, while others take shorter trips of only a few hundred miles.

Baleen whales are among the largest animals that have ever lived. The largest, the blue whale, weighs up to one hundred and sixty tons—as much as twenty-five elephants. Even the smallest baleen whale, the pygmy right whale, weighs five tons—as much as a hippopotamus. As large as baleen whales are, they feed only on krill, tiny shrimplike animals about as big as a person's little finger. The whales filter the krill out of the water using the baleen plates in their mouths.

Most baleen whales breed in warm tropical waters where their calves have a better chance to survive and grow. But tropical waters tend to have less plankton, and less krill, which feed on the plankton. So when the calves are a few months old, the mothers travel with them to colder waters where the plankton and krill are plentiful.

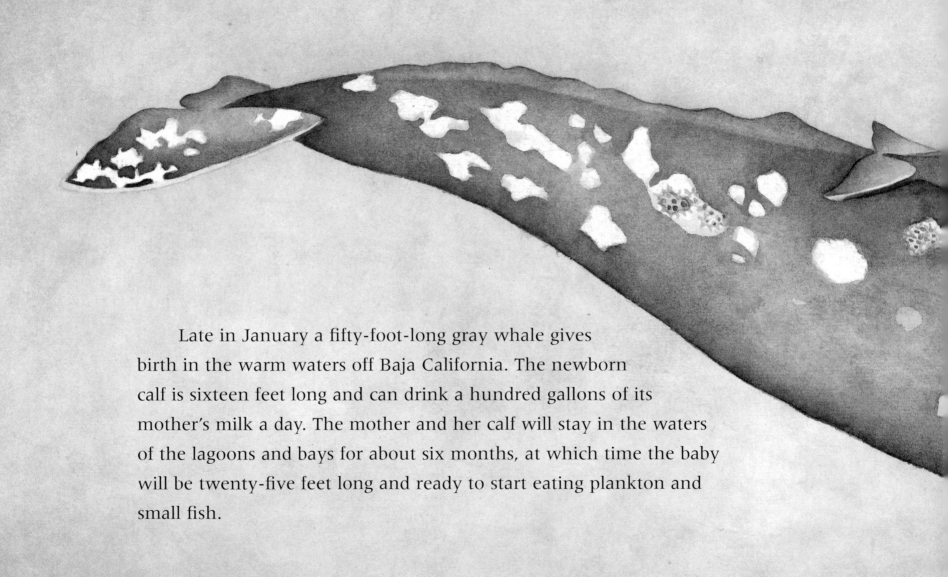

Late in January a fifty-foot-long gray whale gives
birth in the warm waters off Baja California. The newborn
calf is sixteen feet long and can drink a hundred gallons of its
mother's milk a day. The mother and her calf will stay in the waters
of the lagoons and bays for about six months, at which time the baby
will be twenty-five feet long and ready to start eating plankton and
small fish.

Now the mother and her calf will begin to swim northward along the coast of the United States. They will swim four thousand miles from Baja California to the Bering Sea. After several months of feeding in the rich ocean waters of the Bering Sea, the whales will begin their return journey to the south. At one time gray whales migrated north in herds of more than a thousand animals a day. Now only a few thousand are left to make the trip each year.

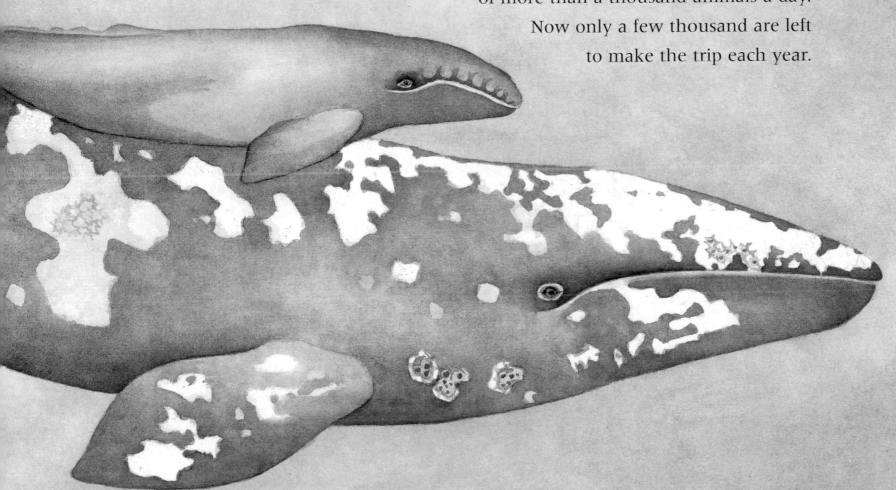

Not all ocean travelers are swimmers. Some *walk* on the sea bottom. In mid-autumn, early seasonal storms that signal the arrival of winter lash the Florida coast. Spiny lobsters living in the blustery waters on the shallow banks off the island of Bimini begin to leave the holes in the reefs in which they spawned during the summer. Soon they form into head-to-tail lines of two to as many as sixty animals, each lobster touching the tail of the one in front of it.

Single file, the line—or queue—of lobsters marches at a quick clip across the ocean floor, moving southwest from the storm-churned, cloudy waters near the Bimini reefs to the crystal clear deeper waters of the Gulf Stream. The lobsters, which may weigh as much as thirty-five pounds, march day and night for several days. Very few lobsters march alone, and those few solitary individuals that do quickly join passing queues.

Now and then a line leader will stop to probe the sand for food. As they wait in the queue, some lobsters also look for food in the sand,

while others dance about from side to side. Each lobster remains in contact with the lobster just ahead. Those who find food use their front two pairs of legs to eat, while their rear three pairs of legs do the walking as the line moves on.

The lines of lobsters are attacked by fish, especially the queen triggerfish, as they travel across the open, sandy ocean floor. The lead lobster responds to an attack by quickly spinning around, causing the other lobsters to wind around it like a coiled chain. When the last lobster is reeled in, the lobsters all face outward or upward, forming a defensive circle of long, horny spines.

After several days only a few lobsters remain near Bimini. The rest drop off from the queues over a twenty- to thirty-mile feeding area that ranges along the edges of the deeper ocean banks. Some lobsters remain here among scattered reefs for the rest of their lives, while others return singly to the shallows off Bimini in the spring and summer. In autumn the walking journey of the lobsters begins again.

MORE ABOUT OCEAN JOURNEYS

Plankton sometimes make horizontal (side-to-side) journeys as well as vertical (up-and-down) ones. The timing and distance of the up-and-down journeys are affected by the amount of available food and by the numbers of predators at different levels in the water. Some plankton journeys are also influenced by the changes in water temperature as they move up and down.

Plant plankton can move up and down by controlling the amount of gas, oil, or salt within their bodies. When they produce lighter gas or reduce the amount of salt, their bodies become more buoyant and they rise in the water. Reversing the process causes them to sink. Some plant plankton also have whiplike hairs (flagella) that help them move up or down. Animal plankton move by swimming with legs, stiff hairs, or fins, and/or by wiggling their whole bodies.

When female green turtles crawl above the tide line on the beach to bury their eggs, they and their eggs are easy prey for animal predators and for humans who hunt the green turtles for their shells, skin, oil, and meat. Because of hunting and because many breeding beaches have been built upon and are no longer available to the turtles, the green turtle, ridley, and leatherback are in danger of extinction.

Depending on the temperature of the sand, green turtle eggs hatch after fifty to seventy days. The temperature of the sand also determines the sex of the baby turtles: Warm nests can produce all female hatchlings, whereas cool nests can produce all males.

Hatchlings seem to be able to locate the sea by the dim glow of light reflected off its surface. That makes the seaward direction brighter than the landward direction even during moonless nights. Scientists have made many discoveries about these sea turtles, but how the turtles can navigate such long distances with such pinpoint accuracy is one of the great mysteries of animal migration.

How eels reproduce has always been a mystery. No female full of eggs has ever been caught, and no one knows why the females move downstream in the autumn. Over time all sorts of fables have arisen as a result of this lack of information. Two thousand years ago, for example, the Greek philosopher Aristotle suggested that eels were born out of mud. A popular medieval myth was that eels came from horse hairs that had fallen into the water. Yet the facts are even more interesting than the myths.

Although we still do not know exactly what happens to eels at sea, the outline is clear. The eels descend to depths of five hundred to twenty-five hundred feet. In huge shoals, eels by the million slowly swim, following ocean currents, to the Sargasso Sea. Scientists think that the trip from Europe takes at least five months, the trip from the Americas somewhat less.

By finding the smallest leaf fish, which may be only hours old, scientists think that spawning takes place in the depths of the Sargasso Sea. The adults then die, as far as we know, and millions of their bodies decay on the ocean floor beneath the seaweed. The fertilized eggs drift to the surface and hatch into young eels. And then the return journey begins.

Drifting westward as they grow, the leaf fish are caught in the currents of the Gulf Stream and are swept along the eastern coast of the United States before turning east to Northern Europe. The American eels ride the Gulf Stream for six to eight months before they turn westward to the coast and transform into glass eels, or elvers. As they move into freshwater rivers, they grow larger, becoming yellow, or juvenile, eels. The European eels stay in the Gulf Stream for two or three years before they reach the coast of Europe and swim into the rivers.

The return of the glass eels to the rivers takes place from autumn to late spring, depending on the place. The glass eels work their way upriver, crawling up and over waterfalls and perhaps even traveling over the land on damp nights. Finally they reach the ponds and lakes where they will grow and become adults. And then the cycle will begin again.

Before laying her eggs a female salmon chooses a place in a rocky stream where there is rapid water circulation. She turns on her side and sweeps her tail rapidly upward, making a nest in the gravel. Then she lays her eggs in the nest, where they are fertilized by a male. The female guards her nest to prevent other females from digging up the eggs. Atlantic salmon return to the sea after spawning and come back in other years to spawn again. But the most numerous kinds of Pacific salmon make the trip only once, and die after they spawn.

What guides the salmon back to its home waters? Scientists think that salmon use both the earth's magnetic field and the sun's position to find their way, and also as a kind of calendar. For example, most of the millions of sockeye salmon that return to Bristol Bay in Alaska arrive within a two-week period in the autumn. It appears that salmon can detect changes in the duration of the daylight, which tells them when it is time to migrate.

On their journey upriver to the stream in which they were born, the salmon may pass many other streams suitable for spawning. Their sense of smell helps them identify their very own spawning stream. Young salmon learn the particular smells of their home stream before they leave on their ocean journeys; they hone in on that smell when they return.

Seals and sea lions belong to a family of animals called pinnipeds, which means "finned feet." These mammals have finned flippers and are adapted to spend part of their lives in water. Unlike whales and porpoises—mammals that live and breed in the ocean—pinnipeds must spend some of their lives on land or on floating ice. Seals and sea lions are not nearly as fast in the water as porpoises and whales, but they can turn and twist more easily and can live safely in the crashing surf around jagged rocks.

Northern fur seals breed on the small, windswept Pribilof Islands in the Bering Sea. Nothing seems to prevent them from returning to the same islands to breed each year, though the animals are hunted and killed there by the thousands for their fur. These seals are herd animals. The males, called bulls, have large harems of forty to fifty females, called cows. Thousands upon thousands of fur seals make up the rookeries where the young are born in the spring.

Whales have been found to have deposits of magnetite in their bodies. Magnetite is a magnetic iron ore that responds to the earth's magnetic field, somewhat like a compass. Some scientists think that whales and other sea animals, such as salmon and turtles, have a magnetic sense that helps them navigate on their long journeys.

Whales face many dangers during their migrations. Why, then, do they undertake these long and difficult journeys? Whales are warm-blooded and need to maintain a constant body temperature. In warm seas their body-heat loss to the surrounding water is much less than in the freezing polar seas.

Newborn whale calves have no insulating layer of fat, called blubber, beneath their skins. If the calves were born in cold polar waters, they would freeze to death very quickly. But the warm tropical waters where birthing occurs are poor in plankton, krill, and other food that the adult whales must eat. So the whales must migrate to areas where krill is plentiful to obtain the vast amounts of food they need.

There are probably hundreds of reasons animals begin the long journeys called migrations. These journeys have evolved over thousands or millions of years in order for the animals to find food for themselves or their offspring, or to find better conditions, or to reproduce in safety. Just as some animals' body shapes or sizes or characteristics help them and their young to survive in their surroundings, so too do the strange long journeys some animals take through the vast oceans of the earth.

The illustrations in this book were done in watercolor on
Fabriano Artistico, 140 lb. cold-press, 100% cotton paper.
The display type was set in Tiepolo Bold.
The text type was set in Meridien.
Color separations by Tien Wah Press, Singapore
Printed and bound by Tien Wah Press, Singapore
This book was printed on totally chlorine-free Nymolla Matte Art paper.
Production supervision by Stanley Redfern
Designed by Judythe Sieck